Elementary Piano Solo with Optional Duet Accompaniment

A Mysterious Night

Martha Mier

A Mysterious Night

Martha Mier

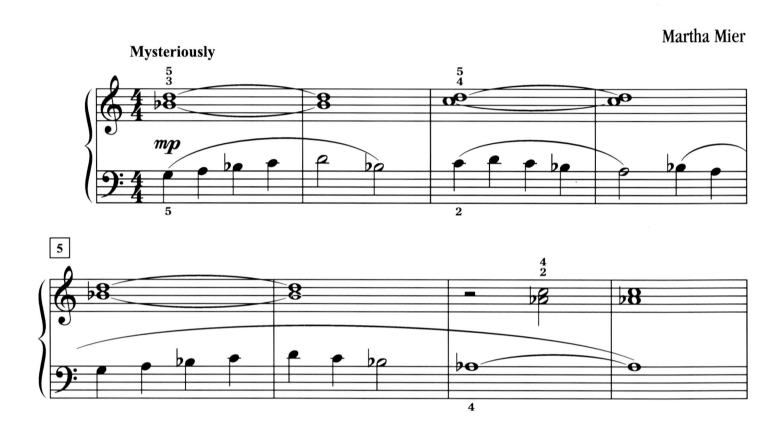

Optional Duet Accompaniment (Student plays one octave higher)

Optional Duet Accompaniment (Continued)

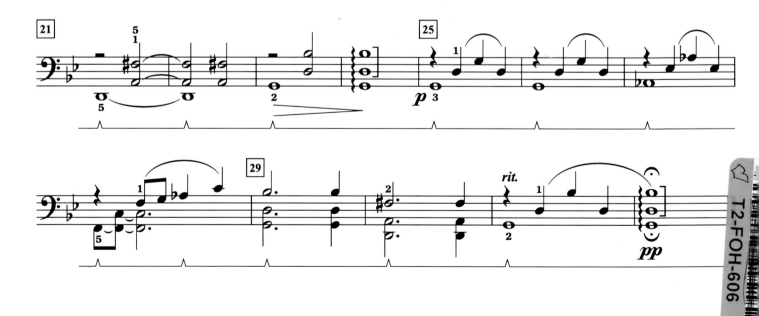

44294 $3.50 in USA

ISBN 1-4706-2038-3

alfred.com

ISBN-10: 1-4706-203_
ISBN-13: 978-1-4706-2038-7

0 38081 49886 7

9 781470 620387